D0643518

Baby Monkeys at the Zoo

Eustacia Moldovo

Enslow Publishing
101 W. 23rd Street
Suite 240
New York, NY 10011
USA

enslow.com

Published in 2016 by Enslow Publishing, LLC.
101 W. 23rd Street, Suite 240, New York, NY 10011

Library of Congress Cataloging-in-Publication Data
Moldovo, Eustacia.
  Baby monkeys at the zoo / Eustacia Moldovo.
    pages cm. — (All about baby zoo animals)
  Audience: Age 4-6.
  Audience: K to Grade 3.
  Includes bibliographical references and index.
  Summary: "Describes the life of a monkey infant at a zoo, including its behaviors, diet, and physical traits"—Provided by publisher.
  ISBN 978-0-7660-7075-2 (library binding)
  ISBN 978-0-7660-7073-8 (pbk.)
  ISBN 978-0-7660-7074-5 (6-pack)
  1. Monkeys—Infancy—Juvenile literature. 2. Zoo animals—Juvenile literature. I. Title.
  QL737.P9M588 2016
  599.8'139—dc23
                    2015000148

Printed in the United States of America

To Our Readers: We have done our best to make sure all Web sites in this book were active and appropriate when we went to press. However, the author and the publisher have no control over and assume no liability for the material available on those Web sites or on any Web sites they may link to. Any comments or suggestions can be sent by e-mail to customerservice@enslow.com.

Photo Credits: bogdan ionescu/Shutterstock.com, pp. 4–5; Cuson/Shutterstock.com, p. 1; defpicture/Shutterstock.com, pp. 3 (left), 8; dmvphotos/Shutterstock.com, p. 10; Els van der Gun/iStock/Thinkstock, p. 22; Eric Gevaert/Shutterstock.com, p. 6; i359702/Shutterstock.com, p. 18; Im Perfect Lazybones/Shutterstock.com, p. 20; JPL Designs/Shutterstock.com, pp. 3 (center), 12; SilvestreSelva/iStock/Thinkstock, p. 14; tratong/Shutterstock.com, pp. 3 (right), 16.

Cover Credits: Els van der Gun/iStock/Thinkstock, p. 22 (baby monkey in hole); Nelson Marques/Shutterstock.com (baby blocks on spine).

Contents

Words to Know

infant   tail   troop

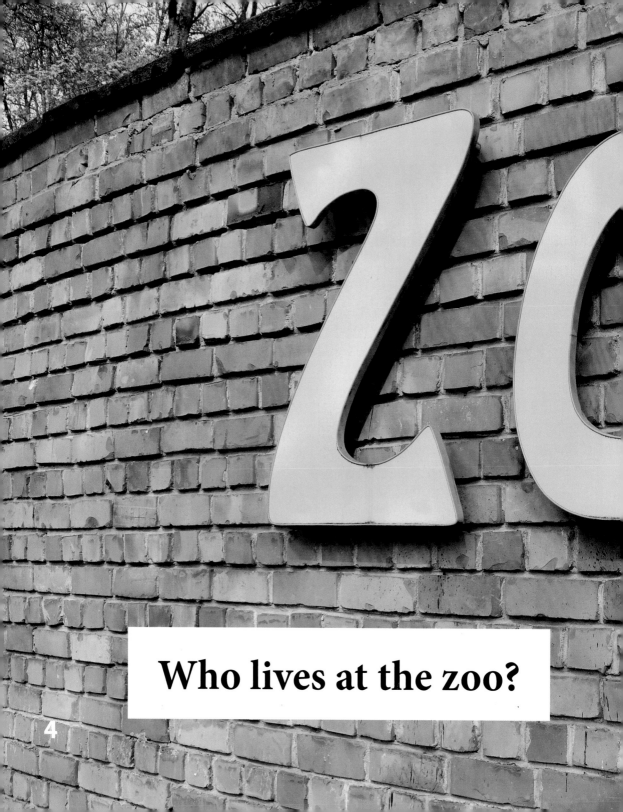

Who lives at the zoo?

A baby monkey lives at the zoo!

A baby monkey is called an infant, just like a human baby!

There are many kinds of monkeys. They can be black, white, gray, brown, orange, and other colors.

This monkey infant has a long tail. The tail helps the monkey pick up things as small as nuts!

A monkey infant rides on its mother's back. The mother carries it around until it can keep up with her.

A monkey infant lives with its family at the zoo. A family of monkeys is called a troop.

A monkey infant eats fruit.
Monkeys also eat nuts,
leaves, seeds, and bugs.

A mother monkey cleans her baby. Cleaning each other is one way monkeys show love!

You can see a monkey infant at the zoo!

Read More

DK Publishing. *Monkeys*. New York: DK Children, 2012.

Schreiber, Anne. *Monkeys*. Des Moines, Iowa: National Geographic Children's Books, 2013.

Web Sites

San Diego Zoo Kids: Capuchin Monkey
kids.sandiegozoo.org/animals/mammals/capuchin-monkey

Science Kids: Fun Monkey Facts for Kids
sciencekids.co.nz/sciencefacts/animals/monkey.html

Index

Guided Reading Level: D
Guided Reading Leveling System is based on the guidelines recommended by Fountas and Pinnell.

Word Count: 135